The Playhouse

The playhouse

Let's pretend the playhouse is a special place.
What could the playhouse be?

Sometimes the playhouse is a café.
Sometimes the playhouse is a hospital.
Sometimes the playhouse is a spaceship.

What other places have you turned your playhouse into?

In this book we turn the playhouse into a nursery for a baby,
and then a greengrocer's shop.

A nursery is a home for a
new baby.
You will help to make the
nursery.
Nurseries are inventions.
Nurseries have inventions.

Next, you can turn the
playhouse into a
greengrocer's shop.
You will make things for
your shop.
You will sell things from
your shop.
Shops are inventions.
Shops have inventions.

A nursery

Rock-a-bye baby, on the tree top,
When the wind blows, the cradle will rock.
When the bough breaks, the cradle will fall,
Down will come baby, cradle and all.

Turn your playhouse into a home for a new baby.

✳ What do babies need?

What kind of inventions are there:

◆ to keep babies warm?
◆ to keep babies comfortable?
◆ to help babies to sleep?
◆ to feed babies?

Collect
Inventions for babies.

Choose one object a day. Talk about why it was invented.
What does it do?

Activity 2

Babies' blankets

You will need

magnifying glass   blankets

What words would you use to describe the blankets?

rough
smooth
holey

stretchy
stiff
cuddly

Which type of material would keep baby warmest?
Use magnifying glasses to look closely at the materials.

Test the blankets.

You will need
lemonade bottles

Use a lemonade bottle
filled with warm water to
be the baby. Wrap several
bottles filled with the
warm water in different
materials.
Which bottle keeps
warmest the longest?

Toys are inventions

Collect

Toys.

We need some toys for the baby. Which would be best?

✳ How do your toys work?

✳ What materials are they made from?

✳ Where will baby use them?

Sort them into different sets.

Your teacher can invite a mother and baby into the classroom. Ask the mother which toys would be best and safest for the baby.

Nappy inventions

How many different kinds of nappies are there?

Collect

different nappies

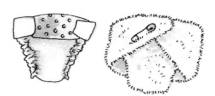

* Which are washable nappies?
* Which are disposable nappies?

What are the good points and bad points of each of these types of nappies?

Invent a test for each nappy. Think about what nappies need to do.

You will need

water · baby-sized doll

Try putting different nappies on the same doll.

Try putting water on each nappy.

Which is the best nappy?

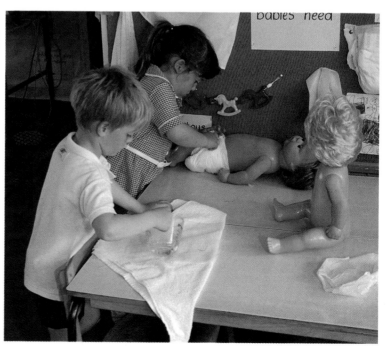

Cribs, cradles and cots

Babies spend a lot of time sleeping.

Can you think of inventions to help baby sleep?

What is a crib?   What is a cradle?   What is a cot?

Here are pictures of a crib, a cradle and a cot.

✳In what ways are they the same?
✳In what ways are they different?

Look at some baby catalogues.

Cut out all the things which will help baby sleep.

Which do you like the best?

Do you know any new babies?

What do they sleep in?

What could they sleep in?

Ideas! Ideas! Ideas!

Paint a picture of baby asleep in your invention.

Inventing a cradle

You will need

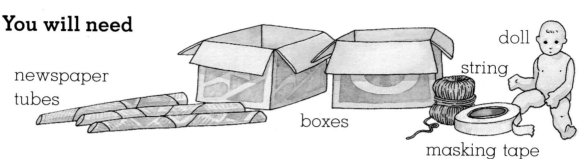

newspaper tubes

boxes

doll

string

masking tape

Talk about the cradle you have to design.

* What does it need to do?
* What size should it be?
* Does it have to be strong?
* How do we support the cradle?

Think up some ideas. Test the best ones.

You could use newspaper tubes. You make these by wrapping newspapers round a dowel.

How will you join the tubes?

Practise tying tubes together with elastic bands.

Practise strapping tubes together.

Testing your cradles

Look at the designs you have made for the cradle.
Talk about them.

* Where will the baby sleep? Would the baby be comfortable?
* How strong is the cradle?
* How safe is the cradle?
* Does the weight push or pull on the structure?
* Does the cradle look attractive?

Test which is the biggest baby you could put in the cradle by using different sized dolls.

Activity 8

Playing in the nursery

Put the baby inventions into the playhouse.

Take it in turns to pretend you are either mummy, daddy, brother or sister to the baby.

Think about baby's day. What does baby do from getting up in the morning until night-time?

Make a flow chart of baby's day.

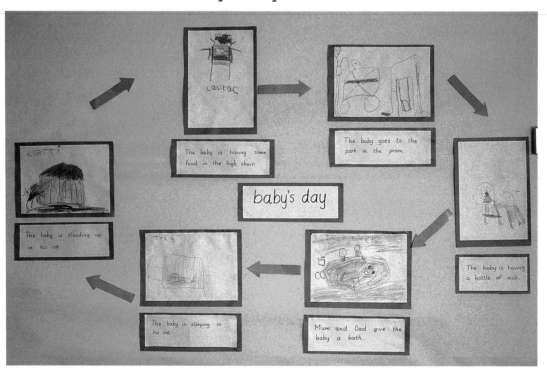

Organise the playhouse so you can bathe, change and feed the baby.

The greengrocer's shop

Let's turn the playhouse into a greengrocer's shop.

Have you been to the greengrocer's?
What goods do greengrocers sell?

We need to design and make
    a plan for the shop.
    goods to sell in the shop.

First, find out about what greengrocers sell.

Collect greengrocer goods

Sort the items into sets of fruits and vegetables.
Sort into other sets.

round shapes

long shapes

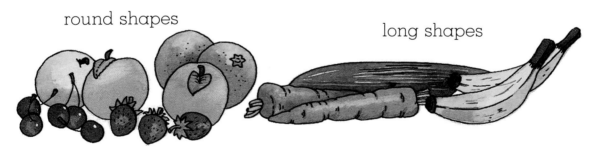

What ideas do you have for sorting into sets?

What do the goods feel
like? Smell like?
Make up some words
to go with your goods.
Which words would
make you want to buy
the goods?

Activity 10

Finding out about fruit

Colour

You will need

sponges   collection of fruit   brushes   paints

Sort all the fruit into sets of colour.

Some things are the same colour but are different shades. They can be

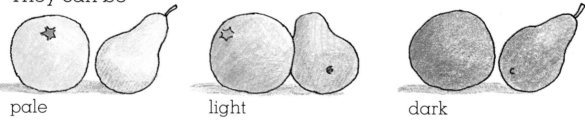

pale   light   dark

Which colour of fruit makes you want to eat it the most?

Paint some fruit.
Try mixing paint. Try different shades of the same colour.

Put the paint on with brushes or sponges.
Can you make patterned fruit?

Leave to dry. Then cut out.

Make a big fruit picture for your classroom wall.

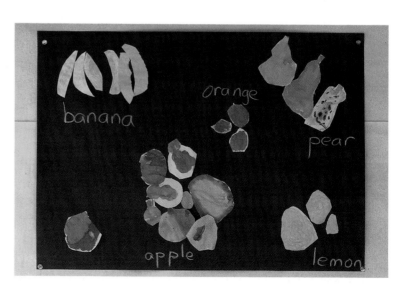

Taste

Which things taste sweet?
Which things taste sour?
What are your favourite tastes?
Have you a 'sweet tooth'?

Tasting Test
You will need

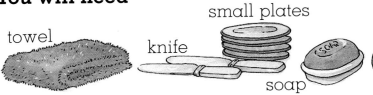

towel   knife   small plates   soap   sweet and sour apples

Some apples are sweet and some are sour.

✳ Which apples look sour?
✳ Which apples look sweet?

Sort into sets.

Do a tasting test.
First of all, make sure everything is clean and safe.
Wash your hands.
Don't taste the fruit if someone else has already.
Let the teacher cut the apples.
Clean the plates and knife.

Be careful

Taste the apples.
✳ Were the sour-looking apples sour?
✳ Were the sweet-looking apples sweet?

Designing and making fruit and vegetables

You will need

dough mixes

The teacher will provide some different types of dough mixes. Feel the dough. Play with it. How does it feel?

Make your own dough mixes.

You will need

food colouring   plain flour   water

salt   tablespoons

Use tablespoons as measures for water and flour. Add some salt. Add colourings, one drop at a time. Find a mix which is just right for making things.

Can you make stiff dough more sloppy?
Can you make sloppy dough more stiff?

Now design some fruit and vegetable shapes using the right colouring.

Invent a new fruit. Make up a name for it.

Working as a team

Problem

You need to make as many apples, bananas or any other fruit as you can in 1 minute. You can work in pairs.

You will need

dough mixes

Take one of your home-made fruit. How can you and your friend make as many as possible?

Think about the problem. How will you share the task?

How many items of fruit did you make? Do you think you could do the task any better or any faster?

Activity 14

Making and testing the shop

Let's make our shop.

You will need

your fruit — small tables — containers

What do we need to think about?

* How do we make the shop look attractive?
  Why does it need to look attractive?
* Where will the shopkeeper stand?
* Where will the customers be?
* Where shall we put the money?

Buy and sell your fruit. Take it in turns to be the shopkeeper and the customer.

Do you like the way you have made your shop?
Is it a good design? What did the customers think?

Have you got any problems?
If yes, try again. If no, well done!